INDIAN DIABETIC COOKBOOK OVER 60

Delicious and Healthy Recipes for Diabetes, Quick and Easy Tasty, All over India

BY

RAJ RAMU

Copyrights 2024 By DR. OLIVIA FAMA All rights reserved worldwide.

No part of this book may be reproduced or transmitted in any form or by any means, electronic or mechanical, including photo-copying, recording or by any information storage and retrieval system, without written permission from the publisher, except for the inclusion of brief quotations in review

Warning-Disclaimer

The purpose of this book is to educate and entertain. The author or publisher does not guarantee that anyone following the techniques, suggestions, tips, ideas, or strategies will become successful. The author and publisher shall have neither liability or responsibility to anyone with respect to any loss or damage caused, or alleged to be caused, directly or indirectly by the information contained in this book

TABLE OF CONTENTS

Introduction: 6
Understanding Diabetes and Nutrition 8
breakfast diabetic recipes designed for individuals over 60 16
   1. Oats Upma 16
   2. Vegetable Dalia (Broken Wheat Porridge) 17
   3. Moong Dal Chilla (Mung Bean Pancake).. 18
   4. Ragi Idli (Finger Millet Steamed Cakes) 20
   5. Methi Paratha (Fenugreek Flatbread) ... 21
   6. Vegetable Uttapam 22
   7. Poha (Flattened Rice) 23
lunch Indian diabetic recipes crafted with the needs of individuals over 60 25
   11. Vegetable Khichdi 25
   12. Palak Paneer (Spinach and Cottage Cheese Curry) 26
   13. Dal Tadka (Tempered Lentils) 27
   14. Methi Matar Malai (Fenugreek and Green Peas Curry) 29
   15. Bharwa Karela (Stuffed Bitter Gourd). 30
   16. Lauki Chana Dal (Bottle Gourd and Bengal Gram Curry) 32
   17. Vegetable Pulao 33
dinner Indian diabetic recipes tailored for individuals over 60 35
   18. Methi Mushroom Curry 35

19. Palak Dal (Spinach Lentil Soup)......... 36
20. Karela Sabzi (Bitter Gourd Stir-fry)..... 37
21. Lauki Sabzi (Bottle Gourd Stir-fry)...... 39
22. Moong Dal Khichdi........................... 40
23. Bhindi Masala (Spicy Okra Stir-fry)..... 41
24. Cabbage Stir-fry.............................. 42
dessert Indian diabetic recipes suitable for individuals over 60... 45
25. Lauki Halwa (Bottle Gourd Pudding)...45
26. Paneer Kheer (Cottage Cheese Pudding)...46
27. Moong Dal Ladoo (Split Mung Bean Sweet Balls)... 47
28. Coconut Barfi................................... 48
29. Besan Ladoo (Chickpea Flour Sweet Balls)... 49
30. Fruit Chaat...................................... 50
31. Yogurt Parfait...................................51
14-day meal plan tailored for Indian diabetic individuals over 60.. 53
WEEK 1..53
WEEK 2..55
CONCLUSION..59
BONUS... 60

Introduction:

In the heart of Mumbai, amidst the bustling streets and vibrant markets, lived Mrs. Patel, a sprightly woman in her late sixties. Her days were filled with the aromatic symphony of spices, the rhythmic clinks of pots and pans, and the laughter of loved ones gathered around her kitchen table. But there was a silent intruder lurking within Mrs. Patel's life, threatening to dim the vibrancy of her days: diabetes.

Like many others in India, Mrs. Patel found herself grappling with the realities of a chronic condition that seemed to touch the lives of more and more individuals with each passing year. The prevalence of diabetes in India had reached alarming levels, affecting millions across generations, with the elderly bearing a particularly heavy burden.

For Mrs. Patel, the diagnosis brought a mix of fear and determination. She knew that managing diabetes wasn't just about controlling blood sugar levels; it was about reclaiming control over her health, her happiness, and her culinary heritage. With the support of her family and a newfound resolve, Mrs. Patel embarked on a journey of discovery, seeking out ways to savor the flavors of her beloved Indian cuisine while safeguarding her well-being.

This journey led Mrs. Patel to uncover a treasure trove of culinary wisdom passed down through generations. She learned that the vibrant tapestry of Indian cuisine was not just a feast for the senses but also a powerful ally in the fight against diabetes. With the guidance of traditional recipes and modern nutritional insights, Mrs. Patel discovered that she could nourish her body and soul without compromising on taste or tradition.

And thus, the idea for this cookbook was born—a celebration of the rich flavors, nourishing ingredients, and time-honored techniques that define Indian cooking, reimagined for those navigating the complexities of diabetes in their golden years. In these pages, you'll find a symphony of spices, a palette of colors, and a world of possibilities, all crafted with love and care to empower you on your own journey towards health and happiness.

Welcome to Flavors of Health: A Diabetic Cookbook for the Indian Elderly. Here, you'll discover more than just recipes; you'll find inspiration, empowerment, and a reminder that with the right ingredients and a sprinkle of determination, every meal can be a step towards a brighter, healthier tomorrow.

Understanding Diabetes and Nutrition

What is Diabetes?

Diabetes mellitus, commonly known as diabetes, is a chronic metabolic disorder characterized by elevated levels of blood glucose (sugar). This condition arises when the body either cannot produce enough insulin—a hormone that regulates blood sugar—or cannot effectively use the insulin it produces.

There are primarily two types of diabetes:

Type 1 Diabetes: This type occurs when the immune system mistakenly attacks and destroys the insulin-producing beta cells in the pancreas. Individuals with type 1 diabetes require lifelong insulin therapy to survive.

Type 2 Diabetes: This is the most common form of diabetes, accounting for the majority of cases worldwide. It develops when the body becomes resistant to insulin or does not produce enough insulin to maintain normal blood sugar levels. Type 2 diabetes is often linked to lifestyle factors such as obesity, poor diet, sedentary behavior, and genetic predisposition.

Causes and Symptoms

The causes of diabetes vary depending on the type:

Type 1 Diabetes: The exact cause of type 1 diabetes is still unknown, but it is believed to involve a combination of genetic susceptibility and environmental triggers, such as viral infections.

Type 2 Diabetes: This type is primarily caused by a combination of genetic factors and lifestyle choices, including poor diet, lack of physical activity, obesity, and stress.

Common symptoms of diabetes include:
- Frequent urination
- Excessive thirst
- Unexplained weight loss
- Fatigue
- Blurred vision
- Slow wound healing
- Tingling or numbness in the hands and feet

The Role of Nutrition in Managing Diabetes

Nutrition plays a crucial role in managing diabetes and preventing complications. A well-balanced diet can help regulate blood sugar levels, improve insulin sensitivity, and reduce the risk of cardiovascular disease, which is a common complication of diabetes.

Key principles of diabetic nutrition include:

Carbohydrate Counting: Carbohydrates have the most significant impact on blood sugar levels. Monitoring carbohydrate intake through carbohydrate counting can help individuals with diabetes manage their blood sugar levels more effectively.

Glycemic Index (GI): The glycemic index is a scale that ranks carbohydrate-containing foods based on how quickly they raise blood sugar levels. Foods with a low GI are digested and absorbed more slowly, leading to gradual increases in blood sugar levels. Choosing foods with a low GI can help stabilize blood sugar levels and prevent spikes and crashes.

Portion Control: Controlling portion sizes is essential for managing calorie intake and blood sugar levels. By practicing portion control, individuals with diabetes can prevent overeating and maintain stable blood sugar levels throughout the day.

By understanding the principles of diabetes and nutrition, individuals can make informed dietary choices to manage their condition effectively and improve their overall health and well-being. In the following chapters, we will explore how traditional Indian cuisine can be adapted to meet the nutritional needs of individuals with diabetes over the age of 60, ensuring that every meal is both delicious and nourishing.

The Indian Kitchen: Essential Ingredients and Cooking Techniques

Step into an Indian kitchen, and you'll be greeted by a symphony of aromas, colors, and flavors—a culinary journey steeped in tradition, culture, and history. At the heart of Indian cuisine lie a plethora of ingredients, each chosen not only for its taste but also for its nutritional value and health benefits.

Key Ingredients and Their Nutritional Benefits

Indian cooking is characterized by its use of spices, pulses, grains, vegetables, and lean proteins, all of which contribute to a diverse and balanced diet. Let's explore some of the essential ingredients and their nutritional benefits:

Spices: From the fiery heat of chili peppers to the earthy warmth of cumin and coriander, Indian cuisine boasts a rich tapestry of spices, each offering unique flavors and health-promoting properties. Spices like turmeric, known for its anti-inflammatory properties, and cinnamon, which may help regulate blood sugar levels, are staples in Indian cooking.

Pulses and Legumes: Lentils, chickpeas, kidney beans, and other pulses are a cornerstone of Indian cuisine, prized for their high protein and fiber content. These plant-based proteins are not only heart-healthy but also help stabilize blood sugar levels, making them an excellent choice for individuals with diabetes.

Whole Grains: Indian cooking incorporates a variety of whole grains such as rice, wheat, millets, and oats, providing essential nutrients like fiber, vitamins, and minerals. Whole grains help promote satiety, regulate digestion, and prevent blood sugar spikes, making them an integral part of a diabetic-friendly diet.

Vegetables: From vibrant greens like spinach and fenugreek to hearty vegetables like potatoes and cauliflower, Indian cuisine celebrates the bounties of the earth. Vegetables are rich in vitamins, minerals, and antioxidants, supporting overall health and well-being while adding depth and flavor to dishes.

Lean Proteins: While Indian cuisine is renowned for its vegetarian offerings, it also includes lean sources of protein such as chicken, fish, and paneer (Indian cottage cheese). These protein-rich ingredients help build and repair tissues, promote muscle health, and regulate blood sugar levels.

Healthy Cooking Techniques

In addition to selecting nutritious ingredients, the way we prepare our meals can significantly impact their healthfulness. Here are some tips for incorporating healthy cooking techniques into your Indian kitchen:

Grilling: Grilling is a fantastic way to cook meats, vegetables, and even paneer without adding excess oil. It imparts a smoky flavor and caramelization to foods, enhancing their taste and texture.

Baking: Baking is a healthier alternative to deep-frying and can be used to prepare everything from savory snacks like samosas to indulgent desserts like cakes and cookies. By using less oil and sugar, baking allows you to enjoy your favorite Indian dishes guilt-free.

Steaming: Steaming is a gentle cooking method that helps retain the natural flavors, colors, and nutrients of foods. Steamed vegetables, dumplings, and fish are not only nutritious but also light and delicious.

Reducing Oil and Sugar While Maintaining Flavor

One of the challenges of adapting Indian recipes for a diabetic-friendly diet is reducing the use of oil and sugar without compromising on flavor. Here are some tips to help you achieve that balance:

Use Healthy Fats: Opt for heart-healthy fats like olive oil, coconut oil, and mustard oil in moderation. These fats add flavor and richness to dishes without significantly impacting blood sugar levels.

Experiment with Natural Sweeteners: Instead of refined sugar, try using natural sweeteners like honey, jaggery (unrefined cane sugar), or stevia in your recipes. These alternatives provide sweetness without causing rapid spikes in blood sugar.

Enhance Flavors with Herbs and Spices: Harness the power of herbs and spices to elevate the taste of your dishes without relying on excessive oil or sugar. Fresh herbs like cilantro, mint, and curry leaves, along with spices like ginger, garlic, and fenugreek, add depth and complexity to your cooking.

By embracing nutrient-rich ingredients, adopting healthy cooking techniques, and making mindful choices about oil and sugar, you can create delicious and diabetes-friendly Indian meals that nourish the body and soul. In the following chapters, we'll delve deeper into specific recipes and meal ideas tailored to the needs of diabetic individuals over the age of 60, ensuring that every bite is a celebration of health and flavor.

breakfast diabetic recipes designed for individuals over 60

1. Oats Upma

Preparation Time: 15 minutes
Nutritional Information (per serving):
  Calories: 200 kcal
  Carbohydrates: 35 g
  Protein: 5 g
  Fat: 4 g
  Fiber: 6 g
Ingredients:
- 1 cup rolled oats
- 1 small onion, finely chopped
- 1 small carrot, grated
- 1/4 cup green peas
- 1 green chili, finely chopped
- 1/2 teaspoon mustard seeds
- 1/2 teaspoon cumin seeds
- 1/4 teaspoon turmeric powder
- Salt to taste
- Fresh coriander leaves for garnish
- 1 tablespoon oil

Instructions:
1. Heat oil in a pan and add mustard seeds and cumin seeds. Let them splutter.
2. Add chopped onion and green chili. Sauté until onions turn translucent.
3. Add grated carrot and green peas. Cook for 2-3 minutes.

4. Add turmeric powder and salt. Mix well.
5. Add rolled oats and stir-fry for 2-3 minutes until oats are lightly roasted.
6. Add 2 cups of water and bring to a boil. Cover and cook on low heat for 5-7 minutes or until oats are cooked and water is absorbed.
7. Garnish with fresh coriander leaves and serve hot.

2. Vegetable Dalia (Broken Wheat Porridge)

Preparation Time: 20 minutes
Nutritional Information (per serving):
  Calories: 180 kcal
  Carbohydrates: 30 g
  Protein: 6 g
  Fat: 4 g
  Fiber: 5 g
Ingredients:
- 1/2 cup broken wheat (dalia)
- 1 small onion, finely chopped
- 1 small tomato, finely chopped
- 1/4 cup mixed vegetables (carrots, peas, beans)
- 1/2 teaspoon ginger-garlic paste
- 1 green chili, finely chopped
- 1/2 teaspoon cumin seeds
- 1/4 teaspoon turmeric powder
- Salt to taste
- Fresh coriander leaves for garnish

- 1 teaspoon oil

Instructions:
1. Heat oil in a pressure cooker and add cumin seeds. Let them splutter.
2. Add chopped onion, green chili, and ginger-garlic paste. Sauté until onions turn golden brown.
3. Add chopped tomatoes and cook until soft.
4. Add mixed vegetables, turmeric powder, and salt. Cook for 2-3 minutes.
5. Add broken wheat and sauté for another 2-3 minutes.
6. Add 2 cups of water and pressure cook for 3-4 whistles or until dalia is cooked.
7. Garnish with fresh coriander leaves and serve hot.

3. Moong Dal Chilla (Mung Bean Pancake)

Preparation Time: 20 minutes
Nutritional Information (per serving):
  Calories: 150 kcal
  Carbohydrates: 20 g
  Protein: 8 g
  Fat: 4 g
  Fiber: 4 g
Ingredients:
- 1/2 cup split moong dal (mung beans), soaked for 2-3 hours
- 1 small onion, finely chopped
- 1 small tomato, finely chopped

- 1 green chili, finely chopped
- 1/2 teaspoon ginger paste
- Salt to taste
- Fresh coriander leaves for garnish
- 1 teaspoon oil for cooking

Instructions:
1. Drain and rinse soaked moong dal. Blend to a smooth batter with minimal water.
2. Transfer the batter to a bowl and add chopped onion, tomato, green chili, ginger paste, and salt. Mix well.
3. Heat a non-stick pan and grease it lightly with oil.
4. Pour a ladleful of batter onto the pan and spread it in a circular motion to make a thin pancake.
5. Cook on medium heat until the edges turn golden brown. Drizzle a few drops of oil on the edges.
6. Flip the chilla and cook on the other side until cooked through.
7. Garnish with fresh coriander leaves and serve hot with chutney or yogurt.

4. Ragi Idli (Finger Millet Steamed Cakes)

Preparation Time: 30 minutes (excluding fermentation time)
Nutritional Information (per serving):
  Calories: 120 kcal
  Carbohydrates: 20 g
  Protein: 5 g

Fat: 2 g
Fiber: 3 g
Ingredients:
- 1 cup ragi (finger millet) flour
- 1/2 cup idli rice
- 1/4 cup urad dal (black gram lentils)
- Salt to taste
- Water as needed

Instructions:
1. Wash and soak idli rice and urad dal separately for 4-6 hours.
2. Grind urad dal to a smooth batter using minimal water. Transfer to a bowl.
3. Grind soaked idli rice to a coarse paste. Mix with urad dal batter.
4. Add ragi flour and salt to the mixture. Mix well to combine.
5. Cover and ferment the batter for 8-10 hours or overnight.
6. Grease idli molds with oil and pour the batter into each mold.
7. Steam in a steamer for 10-12 minutes or until idlis are cooked through.
8. Serve hot with sambar and chutney.

5. Methi Paratha (Fenugreek Flatbread)

Preparation Time: 25 minutes
Nutritional Information (per serving, 1 paratha):
  Calories: 160 kcal
  Carbohydrates: 20 g

Protein: 6 g
Fat: 6 g
Fiber: 4 g
Ingredients:
- 1 cup whole wheat flour
- 1/4 cup fenugreek leaves (methi), finely chopped
- 1 green chili, finely chopped
- 1/2 teaspoon ajwain (carom seeds)
- Salt to taste
- Water as needed
- 1 teaspoon oil for cooking

Instructions:
1. In a mixing bowl, combine whole wheat flour, chopped fenugreek leaves, green chili, ajwain, and salt.
2. Gradually add water and knead into a soft dough. Let it rest for 15 minutes.
3. Divide the dough into equal-sized balls and roll each ball into a flat disc.
4. Heat a non-stick pan and place a rolled paratha on it.
5. Cook for 1-2 minutes on one side, then flip and cook the other side.
6. Drizzle a few drops of oil on both sides and cook until golden brown spots appear.
7. Serve hot with yogurt or pickle.

6. Vegetable Uttapam

Preparation Time: 30 minutes

Nutritional Information (per serving, 2 small uttapams):
- **Calories:** 180 kcal
- **Carbohydrates:** 30 g
- **Protein:** 5 g
- **Fat:** 4 g
- **Fiber:** 5 g

Ingredients:
- 1 cup dosa batter
- 1 small onion, finely chopped
- 1 small tomato, finely chopped
- 1/4 cup mixed vegetables (capsicum, carrot, onion)
- 1 green chili, finely chopped
- Salt to taste
- Fresh coriander leaves for garnish
- 1 teaspoon oil for cooking

Instructions:
1. Heat a non-stick pan and grease it lightly with oil.
2. Pour a ladleful of dosa batter onto the pan and spread it into a thick circle.
3. Sprinkle chopped onion, tomato, mixed vegetables, and green chili on the batter.
4. Press the toppings gently into the batter.
5. Drizzle a few drops of oil around the edges and cook on medium heat until the bottom turns golden brown.
6. Flip the uttapam and cook on the other side until vegetables are cooked through.

7. Garnish with fresh coriander leaves and serve hot with chutney or sambar.

7. Poha (Flattened Rice)

Preparation Time: 20 minutes
Nutritional Information (per serving):
  Calories: 160 kcal
  Carbohydrates: 25 g
  Protein: 3 g
  Fat: 5 g
  Fiber: 2 g
Ingredients:
- 1 cup thick poha (flattened rice)
- 1 small onion, finely chopped
- 1 small potato, boiled and chopped
- 1/4 cup green peas
- 1 green chili, finely chopped
- 1/2 teaspoon mustard seeds
- 1/2 teaspoon cumin seeds
- 1/4 teaspoon turmeric powder
- Salt to taste
- Fresh coriander leaves for garnish
- 1 tablespoon oil

Instructions:
1. Rinse poha under running water until soft. Drain and set aside.
2. Heat oil in a pan and add mustard seeds and cumin seeds. Let them splutter.
3. Add chopped onion and green chili. Sauté until onions turn translucent.

4. Add boiled potato, green peas, turmeric powder, and salt. Cook for 2-3 minutes.
5. Add rinsed poha and mix gently until well combined.
6. Cover and cook on low heat for 5 minutes, allowing the flavors to meld.
7. Garnish with fresh coriander leaves and serve hot with lemon wedges.

These breakfast recipes are not only delicious but also designed to provide essential nutrients while managing blood sugar levels. Enjoy these flavorful dishes as part of a balanced diet tailored to the needs of individuals over 60 with diabetes.

lunch Indian diabetic recipes crafted with the needs of individuals over 60

11. Vegetable Khichdi

Preparation Time: 30 minutes
Nutritional Information (per serving):
  Calories: 250 kcal
  Carbohydrates: 40 g
  Protein: 8 g
  Fat: 6 g
  Fiber: 6 g
Ingredients:
- 1/2 cup rice
- 1/2 cup split moong dal (mung beans)
- 1 carrot, chopped
- 1 potato, diced
- 1/4 cup green peas
- 1 small onion, finely chopped
- 1 tomato, finely chopped
- 1/2 teaspoon cumin seeds
- 1/2 teaspoon turmeric powder
- Salt to taste
- Fresh coriander leaves for garnish
- 1 tablespoon ghee or oil

Instructions:
1. Wash rice and moong dal and soak them in water for 15-20 minutes.
2. Heat ghee or oil in a pressure cooker. Add cumin seeds and let them splutter.

3. Add chopped onion and sauté until golden brown.
4. Add chopped tomato, turmeric powder, and salt. Cook until tomatoes are soft.
5. Add chopped vegetables and cook for 2-3 minutes.
6. Drain water from soaked rice and dal and add them to the pressure cooker.
7. Add 3 cups of water and close the lid. Pressure cook for 3-4 whistles.
8. Once the pressure releases, open the cooker, garnish with fresh coriander leaves, and serve hot.

12. Palak Paneer (Spinach and Cottage Cheese Curry)

Preparation Time: 40 minutes
Nutritional Information (per serving):
  Calories: 280 kcal
  Carbohydrates: 10 g
  Protein: 15 g
  Fat: 20 g
  Fiber: 4 g
Ingredients:
- 2 cups spinach leaves, washed and chopped
- 200 grams paneer (cottage cheese), cubed
- 1 onion, finely chopped
- 2 tomatoes, finely chopped
- 2 green chilies, finely chopped
- 1-inch ginger, grated

- 3 cloves garlic, minced
- 1/2 teaspoon cumin seeds
- 1/2 teaspoon turmeric powder
- 1 teaspoon garam masala
- Salt to taste
- 1 tablespoon oil

Instructions:
1. Heat oil in a pan and add cumin seeds. Let them splutter.
2. Add chopped onion, green chilies, ginger, and garlic. Sauté until onions turn golden brown.
3. Add chopped tomatoes and cook until they turn mushy.
4. Add chopped spinach, turmeric powder, and salt. Cook until spinach wilts.
5. Allow the mixture to cool slightly, then blend it into a smooth paste.
6. Return the mixture to the pan and add paneer cubes and garam masala.
7. Cook for 5-7 minutes until the paneer is heated through.
8. Serve hot with roti or brown rice.

13. Dal Tadka (Tempered Lentils)

Preparation Time: 40 minutes
Nutritional Information (per serving):
   Calories: 220 kcal
   Carbohydrates: 30 g
   Protein: 12 g
   Fat: 6 g

Fiber: 8 g
Ingredients:
- 1/2 cup split pigeon peas (toor dal), washed
- 1/2 cup split moong dal (mung beans), washed
- 1 onion, finely chopped
- 2 tomatoes, finely chopped
- 2 green chilies, slit
- 1-inch ginger, grated
- 3 cloves garlic, minced
- 1/2 teaspoon cumin seeds
- 1/2 teaspoon turmeric powder
- 1 teaspoon garam masala
- Salt to taste
- Fresh coriander leaves for garnish
- 1 tablespoon ghee or oil

Instructions:
1. Pressure cook toor dal and moong dal with 2 cups of water until soft and mushy.
2. Heat ghee or oil in a pan and add cumin seeds. Let them splutter.
3. Add chopped onion, green chilies, ginger, and garlic. Sauté until onions turn golden brown.
4. Add chopped tomatoes and cook until they turn mushy.
5. Add turmeric powder, garam masala, and salt. Mix well.
6. Add cooked dal to the pan and mix thoroughly.

7. Simmer for 5-10 minutes until the flavors meld together.
8. Garnish with fresh coriander leaves and serve hot with rice or roti.

14. Methi Matar Malai (Fenugreek and Green Peas Curry)

Preparation Time: 45 minutes
Nutritional Information (per serving):
  Calories: 280 kcal
  Carbohydrates: 15 g
  Protein: 10 g
  Fat: 20 g
  Fiber: 5 g
Ingredients:
- 1 cup fenugreek leaves (methi), washed and chopped
- 1 cup green peas
- 1 onion, finely chopped
- 1 tomato, finely chopped
- 1/4 cup cashew nuts, soaked in water
- 1/2 cup cream or malai
- 1/2 teaspoon cumin seeds
- 1/2 teaspoon turmeric powder
- 1 teaspoon garam masala
- Salt to taste
- Fresh coriander leaves for garnish
- 1 tablespoon oil

Instructions:
1. Heat oil in a pan and add cumin seeds. Let them splutter.

2. Add chopped onion and sauté until golden brown.
3. Add chopped tomato and cook until soft.
4. Drain water from soaked cashew nuts and add them to the pan. Cook for 2-3 minutes.
5. Allow the mixture to cool slightly, then blend it into a smooth paste.
6. Return the mixture to the pan and add turmeric powder, garam masala, and salt.
7. Add chopped fenugreek leaves and green peas. Cook until the peas are tender.
8. Stir in cream or malai and simmer for 5-7 minutes.
9. Garnish with fresh coriander leaves and serve hot with roti or rice.

15. Bharwa Karela (Stuffed Bitter Gourd)

Preparation Time: 50 minutes
Nutritional Information (per serving):
  Calories: 180 kcal
  Carbohydrates: 10 g
  Protein: 8 g
  Fat: 10 g
  Fiber: 5 g
Ingredients:
- 4 small bitter gourds (karela)
- 1/2 cup gram flour (besan)
- 1 onion, finely chopped
- 1/2 teaspoon cumin seeds
- 1/2 teaspoon turmeric powder
- 1 teaspoon coriander powder

- 1 teaspoon amchur (dry mango powder)
- Salt to taste
- 2 tablespoons oil

Instructions:
1. Wash bitter gourds and slit them lengthwise. Remove the seeds and inner membrane.
2. Rub salt on the inside and outside of the bitter gourds and let them sit for 20 minutes.
3. Meanwhile, prepare the stuffing by mixing gram flour, chopped onion, cumin seeds, turmeric powder, coriander powder, amchur, and salt.
4. Rinse the bitter gourds under running water to remove excess salt. Stuff them with the prepared mixture.
5. Heat oil in a pan and place the stuffed bitter gourds. Cook on low heat, covered, for 15-20 minutes, turning occasionally, until they are tender and golden brown.
6. Serve hot with roti or brown rice.

16. Lauki Chana Dal (Bottle Gourd and Bengal Gram Curry)

Preparation Time: 40 minutes
Nutritional Information (per serving):
  Calories: 220 kcal
  Carbohydrates: 30 g
  Protein: 10 g
  Fat: 6 g

Fiber: 8 g
Ingredients:
- 1 cup bottle gourd (lauki), peeled and chopped
- 1/2 cup Bengal gram (chana dal), soaked for 2-3 hours
- 1 onion, finely chopped
- 2 tomatoes, finely chopped
- 1/2 teaspoon cumin seeds
- 1/2 teaspoon turmeric powder
- 1 teaspoon coriander powder
- 1 teaspoon garam masala
- Salt to taste
- Fresh coriander leaves for garnish
- 1 tablespoon oil

Instructions:
1. Heat oil in a pressure cooker and add cumin seeds. Let them splutter.
2. Add chopped onion and sauté until golden brown.
3. Add chopped tomatoes and cook until they turn mushy.
4. Add chopped bottle gourd, soaked chana dal, turmeric powder, coriander powder, garam masala, and salt. Mix well.
5. Add 2 cups of water and pressure cook for 3-4 whistles.
6. Once the pressure releases, open the cooker, garnish with fresh coriander leaves, and serve hot with rice or roti.

17. Vegetable Pulao

Preparation Time: 40 minutes
Nutritional Information (per serving):
  Calories: 280 kcal
  Carbohydrates: 45 g
  Protein: 8 g
  Fat: 8 g
  Fiber: 6 g

Ingredients:
- 1 cup basmati rice, washed and soaked for 30 minutes
- 1 onion, thinly sliced
- 1 carrot, diced
- 1 potato, diced
- 1/4 cup green peas
- 1/4 cup cauliflower florets
- 1/4 cup green beans, chopped
- 2 cloves garlic, minced
- 1-inch ginger, grated
- 2 green chilies, slit
- 1/2 teaspoon cumin seeds
- 1/2 teaspoon garam masala
- Salt to taste
- Fresh coriander leaves for garnish
- 2 tablespoons ghee or oil

Instructions:
1. Heat ghee or oil in a pressure cooker and add cumin seeds. Let them splutter.
2. Add thinly sliced onion and sauté until golden brown.

3. Add minced garlic, grated ginger, and slit green chilies. Sauté for a minute.
4. Add diced vegetables and cook for 3-4 minutes.
5. Drain water from soaked rice and add it to the pressure cooker.
6. Add garam masala and salt. Mix well.
7. Add 2 cups of water and pressure cook for 2 whistles.
8. Once the pressure releases, open the cooker, fluff the pulao with a fork, garnish with fresh coriander leaves, and serve hot.

These lunch recipes are not only delicious but also designed to provide essential nutrients while managing blood sugar levels. Enjoy these flavorful dishes as part of a balanced diet tailored to the needs of individuals over 60 with diabetes.

dinner Indian diabetic recipes tailored for individuals over 60

18. Methi Mushroom Curry

Preparation Time: 40 minutes
Nutritional Information (per serving):
  Calories: 220 kcal
  Carbohydrates: 15 g
  Protein: 10 g
  Fat: 15 g
  Fiber: 5 g
Ingredients:
- 200 grams mushrooms, sliced
- 1 cup fenugreek leaves (methi), chopped
- 1 onion, finely chopped
- 2 tomatoes, finely chopped
- 2 cloves garlic, minced
- 1-inch ginger, grated
- 1/2 teaspoon cumin seeds
- 1/2 teaspoon turmeric powder
- 1 teaspoon coriander powder
- 1 teaspoon garam masala
- Salt to taste
- Fresh coriander leaves for garnish
- 1 tablespoon oil

Instructions:
1. Heat oil in a pan and add cumin seeds. Let them splutter.

2. Add chopped onion, garlic, and ginger. Sauté until onions turn golden brown.
3. Add chopped tomatoes and cook until soft.
4. Add sliced mushrooms and chopped fenugreek leaves. Cook for 5-7 minutes.
5. Add turmeric powder, coriander powder, garam masala, and salt. Mix well.
6. Cook for another 5-7 minutes until the mushrooms are tender and the flavors meld together.
7. Garnish with fresh coriander leaves and serve hot with roti or brown rice.

19. Palak Dal (Spinach Lentil Soup)

Preparation Time: 30 minutes
Nutritional Information (per serving):
Calories: 180 kcal
Carbohydrates: 25 g
Protein: 10 g
Fat: 5 g
Fiber: 8 g
Ingredients:
- 1/2 cup split pigeon peas (toor dal), washed
- 2 cups spinach leaves, washed and chopped
- 1 onion, finely chopped
- 2 tomatoes, finely chopped
- 2 green chilies, slit
- 1-inch ginger, grated

- 1/2 teaspoon cumin seeds
- 1/2 teaspoon turmeric powder
- Salt to taste
- Fresh coriander leaves for garnish
- 1 tablespoon oil

Instructions:
1. Pressure cook toor dal with 2 cups of water until soft and mushy.
2. Heat oil in a pan and add cumin seeds. Let them splutter.
3. Add chopped onion, green chilies, and ginger. Sauté until onions turn golden brown.
4. Add chopped tomatoes and cook until they turn mushy.
5. Add chopped spinach and cook until wilted.
6. Add cooked dal, turmeric powder, and salt. Mix well.
7. Simmer for 5-10 minutes until the flavors meld together.
8. Garnish with fresh coriander leaves and serve hot with rice or roti.

20. Karela Sabzi (Bitter Gourd Stir-fry)

Preparation Time: 30 minutes
Nutritional Information (per serving):
　Calories: 120 kcal
　Carbohydrates: 10 g
　Protein: 5 g
　Fat: 8 g

Fiber: 6 g
Ingredients:
- 4 small bitter gourds (karela), thinly sliced
- 1 onion, thinly sliced
- 2 tomatoes, finely chopped
- 2 green chilies, slit
- 1/2 teaspoon cumin seeds
- 1/2 teaspoon turmeric powder
- 1 teaspoon coriander powder
- 1 teaspoon amchur (dry mango powder)
- Salt to taste
- Fresh coriander leaves for garnish
- 1 tablespoon oil

Instructions:
1. Heat oil in a pan and add cumin seeds. Let them splutter.
2. Add thinly sliced onion and sauté until golden brown.
3. Add sliced bitter gourd and cook on low heat until they are slightly tender.
4. Add chopped tomatoes, green chilies, turmeric powder, coriander powder, amchur, and salt. Mix well.
5. Cover and cook for 10-15 minutes until the bitter gourd is fully cooked and the flavors meld together.
6. Garnish with fresh coriander leaves and serve hot with roti or brown rice.

21. Lauki Sabzi (Bottle Gourd Stir-fry)

Preparation Time: 30 minutes
Nutritional Information (per serving):
  Calories: 100 kcal
  Carbohydrates: 15 g
  Protein: 3 g
  Fat: 4 g
  Fiber: 4 g

Ingredients:
- 2 cups bottle gourd (lauki), peeled and diced
- 1 onion, finely chopped
- 2 tomatoes, finely chopped
- 2 green chilies, slit
- 1/2 teaspoon cumin seeds
- 1/2 teaspoon turmeric powder
- 1 teaspoon coriander powder
- Salt to taste
- Fresh coriander leaves for garnish
- 1 tablespoon oil

Instructions:
1. Heat oil in a pan and add cumin seeds. Let them splutter.
2. Add chopped onion and sauté until golden brown.
3. Add chopped tomatoes and cook until they turn mushy.
4. Add diced bottle gourd and green chilies. Cook on low heat until the bottle gourd is tender.

5. Add turmeric powder, coriander powder, and salt. Mix well.
6. Cover and cook for 10-15 minutes until the flavors meld together.
7. Garnish with fresh coriander leaves and serve hot with roti or brown rice.

22. Moong Dal Khichdi

Preparation Time: 30 minutes
Nutritional Information (per serving):
  Calories: 220 kcal
  Carbohydrates: 35 g
  Protein: 10 g
  Fat: 5 g
  Fiber: 6 g
Ingredients:
- 1/2 cup rice
- 1/2 cup split moong dal (mung beans)
- 1 carrot, diced
- 1 potato, diced
- 1/4 cup green peas
- 1 small onion, finely chopped
- 2 tomatoes, finely chopped
- 1/2 teaspoon cumin seeds
- 1/2 teaspoon turmeric powder
- Salt to taste
- Fresh coriander leaves for garnish
- 1 tablespoon ghee or oil

Instructions:
1. Wash rice and moong dal and soak them in water for 15-20 minutes.

2. Heat ghee or oil in a pressure cooker. Add cumin seeds and let them splutter.
3. Add chopped onion and sauté until golden brown.
4. Add chopped tomatoes and cook until they turn mushy.
5. Add diced vegetables, turmeric powder, and salt. Cook for 2-3 minutes.
6. Drain water from soaked rice and dal and add them to the pressure cooker.
7. Add 3 cups of water and pressure cook for 3-4 whistles.
8. Once the pressure releases, open the cooker, garnish with fresh coriander leaves, and serve hot.

23. Bhindi Masala (Spicy Okra Stir-fry)

Preparation Time: 30 minutes
Nutritional Information (per serving):
   Calories: 150 kcal
   Carbohydrates: 15 g
   Protein: 5 g
   Fat: 8 g
   Fiber: 6 g
Ingredients:
- 2 cups okra (bhindi), washed and chopped
- 1 onion, thinly sliced
- 2 tomatoes, finely chopped
- 2 green chilies, slit
- 1/2 teaspoon cumin seeds

- 1/2 teaspoon turmeric powder
- 1 teaspoon coriander powder
- 1/2 teaspoon red chili powder
- Salt to taste
- Fresh coriander leaves for garnish
- 1 tablespoon oil

Instructions:
1. Heat oil in a pan and add cumin seeds. Let them splutter.
2. Add thinly sliced onion and sauté until golden brown.
3. Add chopped tomatoes and cook until they turn mushy.
4. Add chopped okra and green chilies. Cook on low heat until the okra is tender.
5. Add turmeric powder, coriander powder, red chili powder, and salt. Mix well.
6. Cover and cook for 10-15 minutes until the flavors meld together.
7. Garnish with fresh coriander leaves and serve hot with roti or brown rice.

24. Cabbage Stir-fry

Preparation Time: 25 minutes
Nutritional Information (per serving):
- **Calories:** 100 kcal
- **Carbohydrates:** 10 g
- **Protein:** 3 g
- **Fat:** 6 g
- **Fiber:** 5 g

Ingredients:

- 3 cups cabbage, thinly sliced
- 1 onion, thinly sliced
- 1 tomato, finely chopped
- 2 green chilies, slit
- 1/2 teaspoon cumin seeds
- 1/2 teaspoon mustard seeds
- 1/2 teaspoon turmeric powder
- Salt to taste
- Fresh coriander leaves for garnish
- 1 tablespoon oil

Instructions:
1. Heat oil in a pan and add cumin seeds and mustard seeds. Let them splutter.
2. Add thinly sliced onion and sauté until golden brown.
3. Add chopped tomato and cook until soft.
4. Add thinly sliced cabbage and green chilies. Cook on low heat until the cabbage is tender.
5. Add turmeric powder and salt. Mix well.
6. Cover and cook for 10-15 minutes until the flavors meld together.
7. Garnish with fresh coriander leaves and serve hot with roti or brown rice.

These dinner recipes are not only flavorful but also designed to provide essential nutrients while managing blood sugar levels. Enjoy these delicious dishes as part of a balanced diet tailored to the needs of individuals over 60 with diabetes.

dessert Indian diabetic recipes suitable for individuals over 60

25. Lauki Halwa (Bottle Gourd Pudding)

Preparation Time: 45 minutes
Nutritional Information (per serving):
  Calories: 120 kcal
  Carbohydrates: 20 g
  Protein: 2 g
  Fat: 4 g
  Fiber: 2 g
Ingredients:
- 2 cups grated bottle gourd (lauki)
- 1 cup low-fat milk
- 2 tablespoons ghee (clarified butter)
- 1/4 cup stevia or sugar substitute
- 1/4 teaspoon cardamom powder
- 2 tablespoons chopped nuts (almonds, cashews, pistachios)
- 1 tablespoon raisins

Instructions:
1. Heat ghee in a pan and add grated bottle gourd. Cook on medium heat until it softens.
2. Add low-fat milk and simmer until the mixture thickens, stirring occasionally.
3. Add stevia (or sugar substitute) and cardamom powder. Mix well.
4. Continue cooking until the mixture reaches a halwa-like consistency.

5. Add chopped nuts and raisins. Mix well and cook for another 2-3 minutes.
6. Remove from heat and serve warm or chilled.

26. Paneer Kheer (Cottage Cheese Pudding)

Preparation Time: 30 minutes
Nutritional Information (per serving):
  Calories: 150 kcal
  Carbohydrates: 10 g
  Protein: 8 g
  Fat: 8 g
  Fiber: 0 g
Ingredients:
- 1 liter low-fat milk
- 200 grams paneer (cottage cheese), crumbled
- 1/4 cup stevia or sugar substitute
- 1/4 teaspoon cardamom powder
- 2 tablespoons chopped nuts (almonds, cashews, pistachios)
- Saffron strands for garnish (optional)

Instructions:
1. Heat low-fat milk in a heavy-bottomed pan and bring it to a boil.
2. Reduce the heat and simmer until the milk reduces to half its volume, stirring occasionally.

3. Add crumbled paneer and continue cooking for 5-7 minutes, stirring continuously.
4. Add stevia (or sugar substitute) and cardamom powder. Mix well.
5. Cook for another 2-3 minutes until the kheer thickens slightly.
6. Remove from heat and garnish with chopped nuts and saffron strands.
7. Serve warm or chilled.

27. Moong Dal Ladoo (Split Mung Bean Sweet Balls)

Preparation Time: 40 minutes
Nutritional Information (per serving, 1 ladoo):
  Calories: 90 kcal
  Carbohydrates: 12 g
  Protein: 4 g
  Fat: 3 g
  Fiber: 1 g
Ingredients:
- 1 cup split moong dal (mung beans), roasted
- 1/4 cup stevia or sugar substitute
- 2 tablespoons ghee (clarified butter)
- 1/4 teaspoon cardamom powder
- Chopped nuts for garnish (optional)

Instructions:

1. Dry roast split moong dal until golden brown and aromatic. Allow it to cool completely.
2. Grind the roasted moong dal into a fine powder using a grinder or food processor.
3. Heat ghee in a pan and add the powdered moong dal. Cook on low heat for 8-10 minutes, stirring continuously.
4. Add stevia (or sugar substitute) and cardamom powder. Mix well.
5. Continue cooking until the mixture comes together like a dough.
6. Remove from heat and allow it to cool slightly.
7. Shape the mixture into small ladoos (sweet balls) while still warm.
8. Garnish with chopped nuts if desired.
9. Let the ladoos cool completely before serving.

28. Coconut Barfi

Preparation Time: 40 minutes
Nutritional Information (per serving, 1 piece):
  Calories: 100 kcal
  Carbohydrates: 8 g
  Protein: 2 g
  Fat: 7 g
  Fiber: 1 g
Ingredients:
- 1 cup desiccated coconut
- 1/2 cup low-fat milk

- 1/4 cup stevia or sugar substitute
- 2 tablespoons ghee (clarified butter)
- 1/4 teaspoon cardamom powder
- Chopped nuts for garnish (optional)

Instructions:
1. Heat ghee in a non-stick pan and add desiccated coconut. Roast on low heat until golden brown and aromatic.
2. Add low-fat milk and cook until the mixture thickens, stirring continuously.
3. Add stevia (or sugar substitute) and cardamom powder. Mix well.
4. Continue cooking until the mixture comes together and leaves the sides of the pan.
5. Transfer the mixture to a greased plate and spread it evenly using a spatula.
6. Garnish with chopped nuts if desired, pressing them lightly into the mixture.
7. Allow it to cool completely, then cut into squares or diamonds.
8. Serve at room temperature.

29. Besan Ladoo (Chickpea Flour Sweet Balls)

Preparation Time: 30 minutes
Nutritional Information (per serving, 1 ladoo):
   Calories: 100 kcal
   Carbohydrates: 10 g
   Protein: 3 g
   Fat: 5 g

Fiber: 1 g
Ingredients:
- 1 cup chickpea flour (besan)
- 1/4 cup stevia or sugar substitute
- 2 tablespoons ghee (clarified butter)
- 1/4 teaspoon cardamom powder
- Chopped nuts for garnish (optional)

Instructions:
1. Heat ghee in a non-stick pan and add chickpea flour. Roast on low heat until golden brown and aromatic.
2. Add stevia (or sugar substitute) and cardamom powder. Mix well.
3. Continue roasting until the mixture turns slightly darker in color and gives off a nutty aroma.
4. Remove from heat and allow it to cool slightly.
5. While still warm, shape the mixture into small ladoos (sweet balls) using your hands.
6. Garnish with chopped nuts if desired.
7. Let the ladoos cool completely before serving.

30. Fruit Chaat

Preparation Time: 15 minutes
Nutritional Information (per serving):
  Calories: 80 kcal
  Carbohydrates: 20 g
  Protein: 1 g
  Fat: 0 g

Fiber: 3 g
Ingredients:
- 1 cup mixed fruits (apple, pear, orange, pomegranate)
- 1/2 teaspoon chaat masala
- 1/4 teaspoon black salt
- 1/4 teaspoon roasted cumin powder
- 1 tablespoon lemon juice
- Fresh mint leaves for garnish

Instructions:
1. Peel and chop the fruits into bite-sized pieces.
2. In a large mixing bowl, combine the chopped fruits, chaat masala, black salt, roasted cumin powder, and lemon juice. Toss gently to coat the fruits evenly.
3. Transfer the fruit chaat to serving bowls and garnish with fresh mint leaves.
4. Serve immediately as a refreshing dessert.

31. Yogurt Parfait

Preparation Time: 10 minutes
Nutritional Information (per serving):
   Calories: 120 kcal
   Carbohydrates: 15 g
   Protein: 8 g
   Fat: 3 g
   Fiber: 2 g
Ingredients:
- 1/2 cup low-fat yogurt

- 1/4 cup mixed fruits (berries, kiwi, banana)
- 2 tablespoons granola
- 1 tablespoon chopped nuts (almonds, walnuts)
- 1 teaspoon honey or sugar-free syrup

Instructions:
1. In a serving glass or bowl, layer low-fat yogurt, mixed fruits, granola, and chopped nuts.
2. Drizzle honey or sugar-free syrup on top.
3. Repeat the layers if desired.
4. Serve immediately as a healthy and satisfying dessert option.

These dessert recipes offer delicious and satisfying options for individuals over 60 with diabetes. Enjoy these treats in moderation as part of a balanced diet.

14-day meal plan tailored for Indian diabetic individuals over 60.

WEEK 1

Day 1:
Breakfast:
- Vegetable Dalia (Broken Wheat Porridge)

Lunch:
- Methi Matar Malai (Fenugreek and Green Peas Curry) with Brown Rice

Dinner:
- Palak Dal (Spinach Lentil Soup) with Roti

Day 2:

Breakfast:
- Moong Dal Chilla (Mung Bean Pancakes) with Mint Chutney

Lunch:
- Bhindi Masala (Spicy Okra Stir-fry) with Quinoa

Dinner:
- Lauki Chana Dal (Bottle Gourd and Bengal Gram Curry) with Roti

Day 3:

Breakfast:
- Vegetable Upma (Semolina Porridge) with Coconut Chutney

Lunch:
- Vegetable Pulao with Raita (Yogurt Dip)

Dinner:
- Karela Sabzi (Bitter Gourd Stir-fry) with Brown Rice

Day 4:

Breakfast:
- Besan Chilla (Chickpea Flour Pancakes) with Green Chutney

Lunch:
- Palak Paneer (Spinach and Cottage Cheese Curry) with Quinoa

Dinner:
- Dal Tadka (Tempered Lentils) with Roti

Day 5:

Breakfast:
- Vegetable Poha (Flattened Rice) with a sprinkle of peanuts

Lunch:
- Cabbage Stir-fry with Brown Rice

Dinner:
- Lauki Halwa (Bottle Gourd Pudding)

Day 6:

Breakfast:
- Ragi Dosa (Finger Millet Crepes) with Tomato Chutney

Lunch:
- Moong Dal Khichdi with a side of cucumber salad

Dinner:
- Methi Mushroom Curry with Roti

Day 7:

Breakfast:
- Oats Upma (Savory Oats Porridge) with a dash of lemon

Lunch:
- Paneer Bhurji (Scrambled Cottage Cheese) with Roti

Dinner:
- Vegetable Soup with a side of Multigrain Bread

WEEK 2

Day 8:

Breakfast:
- Sprouts Chaat (Mixed Bean Salad) with a squeeze of lime

Lunch:
- Lauki Sabzi (Bottle Gourd Stir-fry) with Quinoa

Dinner:
- Palak Dal (Spinach Lentil Soup) with Roti

Day 9:

Breakfast:
- Vegetable Uttapam (Savory Rice Pancakes) with Coconut Chutney

Lunch:
- Mixed Vegetable Curry with Brown Rice

Dinner:
- Bharwa Karela (Stuffed Bitter Gourd) with Roti

Day 10:

Breakfast:
- Whole Wheat Dosa with Mint Chutney

Lunch:
- Dal Makhani (Creamy Lentils) with Quinoa

Dinner:
- Bhindi Masala (Spicy Okra Stir-fry) with Brown Rice

Day 11:

Breakfast:
- Vegetable Upma (Semolina Porridge) with a sprinkle of peanuts

Lunch:
- Palak Paneer (Spinach and Cottage Cheese Curry) with Quinoa

Dinner:
- Methi Matar Malai (Fenugreek and Green Peas Curry) with Roti

Day 12:

Breakfast:
- Besan Chilla (Chickpea Flour Pancakes) with Green Chutney

Lunch:
- Cabbage Stir-fry with Brown Rice

Dinner:
- Lauki Chana Dal (Bottle Gourd and Bengal Gram Curry) with Roti

Day 13:

Breakfast:
- Ragi Dosa (Finger Millet Crepes) with Tomato Chutney

Lunch:
- Vegetable Pulao with Raita (Yogurt Dip)

Dinner:
- Karela Sabzi (Bitter Gourd Stir-fry) with Brown Rice

Day 14:

Breakfast:
- Oats Upma (Savory Oats Porridge) with a dash of lemon

Lunch:
- Paneer Bhurji (Scrambled Cottage Cheese) with Roti

Dinner:
- Dal Tadka (Tempered Lentils) with Roti

Feel free to adjust portion sizes and ingredients according to personal preferences and dietary requirements. This meal plan provides a variety of flavors and nutrients while being mindful of managing blood sugar levels effectively.

CONCLUSION

Managing diabetes is not merely a matter of restricting oneself from certain foods; it's about embracing a lifestyle that promotes overall well-being while effectively controlling blood sugar levels. Throughout this journey, we've explored the rich tapestry of Indian cuisine, weaving together traditional flavors with modern nutritional insights to create a diabetic-friendly culinary experience tailored for individuals over 60.

From hearty breakfasts to wholesome lunches, comforting dinners, and delightful desserts, each meal has been thoughtfully crafted to strike a balance between taste, nutrition, and blood sugar management. By incorporating ingredients rich in fiber, lean proteins, and healthy fats, we've ensured that every bite not only satisfies the palate but also nourishes the body.

Beyond the recipes themselves, this journey has emphasized the importance of understanding diabetes, making informed dietary choices, and cultivating healthy cooking habits. By embracing the principles of portion control, mindful eating, and regular physical activity, individuals can take proactive steps towards better health and improved quality of life.

As we bid farewell to these pages, let us carry forward the lessons learned and the flavors savored, infusing our kitchens with creativity, compassion, and culinary wisdom. May each meal be a celebration of life, a testament to resilience, and a reminder that with dedication, determination, and a dash of spice, managing diabetes can be a journey filled with joy, vitality, and delicious possibilities. Here's to health, happiness, and the vibrant flavors of India's diabetic cookbook over 60.

BONUS

MEALS PLANNER JOURNAL

WEEKLY MEAL PLANNING

Month: _____
Week: _____
(1)(2)(3)(4)

Sunday
Breakfast: _____
Calories Protein Sugar Carbs

Lunch: _____
Calories Protein Sugar Carbs

Dinner: _____
Calories Protein Sugar Carbs

Monday
Breakfast: _____
Calories Protein Sugar Carbs

Lunch: _____
Calories Protein Sugar Carbs

Dinner: _____
Calories Protein Sugar Carbs

Tuesday
Breakfast: _____
Calories Protein Sugar Carbs

Lunch: _____
Calories Protein Sugar Carbs

Dinner: _____
Calories Protein Sugar Carbs

Wednesday
Breakfast: _____
Calories Protein Sugar Carbs

Lunch: _____
Calories Protein Sugar Carbs

Dinner: _____
Calories Protein Sugar Carbs

Thursday
Breakfast: _____
Calories Protein Sugar Carbs

Lunch: _____
Calories Protein Sugar Carbs

Dinner: _____
Calories Protein Sugar Carbs

Friday
Breakfast: _____
Calories Protein Sugar Carbs

Lunch: _____
Calories Protein Sugar Carbs

Dinner: _____
Calories Protein Sugar Carbs

Saturday
Breakfast: _____
Calories Protein Sugar Carbs

Lunch: _____
Calories Protein Sugar Carbs

Dinner: _____
Calories Protein Sugar Carbs

Shopping List:
_____
_____
_____
_____
_____
_____
_____
_____

Noted:

WEEKLY MEAL PLANNING

Month: _____
Week: ① ② ③ ④

Sunday
Breakfast: _____
Calories Protein Sugar Carbs

Lunch: _____
Calories Protein Sugar Carbs

Dinner: _____
Calories Protein Sugar Carbs

Monday
Breakfast: _____
Calories Protein Sugar Carbs

Lunch: _____
Calories Protein Sugar Carbs

Dinner: _____
Calories Protein Sugar Carbs

Tuesday
Breakfast: _____
Calories Protein Sugar Carbs

Lunch: _____
Calories Protein Sugar Carbs

Dinner: _____
Calories Protein Sugar Carbs

Wednesday
Breakfast: _____
Calories Protein Sugar Carbs

Lunch: _____
Calories Protein Sugar Carbs

Dinner: _____
Calories Protein Sugar Carbs

Thursday
Breakfast: _____
Calories Protein Sugar Carbs

Lunch: _____
Calories Protein Sugar Carbs

Dinner: _____
Calories Protein Sugar Carbs

Friday
Breakfast: _____
Calories Protein Sugar Carbs

Lunch: _____
Calories Protein Sugar Carbs

Dinner: _____
Calories Protein Sugar Carbs

Saturday
Breakfast: _____
Calories Protein Sugar Carbs

Lunch: _____
Calories Protein Sugar Carbs

Dinner: _____
Calories Protein Sugar Carbs

Shopping List:

Noted:

WEEKLY MEAL PLANNING

Month:
Week:
① ② ③ ④

Sunday
Breakfast:
Calories Protein Sugar Carbs

Lunch:
Calories Protein Sugar Carbs

Dinner:
Calories Protein Sugar Carbs

Monday
Breakfast:
Calories Protein Sugar Carbs

Lunch:
Calories Protein Sugar Carbs

Dinner:
Calories Protein Sugar Carbs

Tuesday
Breakfast:
Calories Protein Sugar Carbs

Lunch:
Calories Protein Sugar Carbs

Dinner:
Calories Protein Sugar Carbs

Wednesday
Breakfast:
Calories Protein Sugar Carbs

Lunch:
Calories Protein Sugar Carbs

Dinner:
Calories Protein Sugar Carbs

Thursday
Breakfast:
Calories Protein Sugar Carbs

Lunch:
Calories Protein Sugar Carbs

Dinner:
Calories Protein Sugar Carbs

Friday
Breakfast:
Calories Protein Sugar Carbs

Lunch:
Calories Protein Sugar Carbs

Dinner:
Calories Protein Sugar Carbs

Saturday
Breakfast:
Calories Protein Sugar Carbs

Lunch:
Calories Protein Sugar Carbs

Dinner:
Calories Protein Sugar Carbs

Shopping List:

Noted:

WEEKLY MEAL PLANNING

Month: _____
Week: _____
(1) (2) (3) (4)

Sunday
Breakfast: _____
Calories | Protein | Sugar | Carbs

Lunch: _____
Calories | Protein | Sugar | Carbs

Dinner: _____
Calories | Protein | Sugar | Carbs

Monday
Breakfast: _____
Calories | Protein | Sugar | Carbs

Lunch: _____
Calories | Protein | Sugar | Carbs

Dinner: _____
Calories | Protein | Sugar | Carbs

Tuesday
Breakfast: _____
Calories | Protein | Sugar | Carbs

Lunch: _____
Calories | Protein | Sugar | Carbs

Dinner: _____
Calories | Protein | Sugar | Carbs

Wednesday
Breakfast: _____
Calories | Protein | Sugar | Carbs

Lunch: _____
Calories | Protein | Sugar | Carbs

Dinner: _____
Calories | Protein | Sugar | Carbs

Thursday
Breakfast: _____
Calories | Protein | Sugar | Carbs

Lunch: _____
Calories | Protein | Sugar | Carbs

Dinner: _____
Calories | Protein | Sugar | Carbs

Friday
Breakfast: _____
Calories | Protein | Sugar | Carbs

Lunch: _____
Calories | Protein | Sugar | Carbs

Dinner: _____
Calories | Protein | Sugar | Carbs

Saturday
Breakfast: _____
Calories | Protein | Sugar | Carbs

Lunch: _____
Calories | Protein | Sugar | Carbs

Dinner: _____
Calories | Protein | Sugar | Carbs

Shopping List:

Noted:

WEEKLY MEAL PLANNING

Month: _____
Week: _____
① ② ③ ④

Sunday
Breakfast: _____
Calories | Protein | Sugar | Carbs

Lunch: _____
Calories | Protein | Sugar | Carbs

Dinner: _____
Calories | Protein | Sugar | Carbs

Monday
Breakfast: _____
Calories | Protein | Sugar | Carbs

Lunch: _____
Calories | Protein | Sugar | Carbs

Dinner: _____
Calories | Protein | Sugar | Carbs

Tuesday
Breakfast: _____
Calories | Protein | Sugar | Carbs

Lunch: _____
Calories | Protein | Sugar | Carbs

Dinner: _____
Calories | Protein | Sugar | Carbs

Wednesday
Breakfast: _____
Calories | Protein | Sugar | Carbs

Lunch: _____
Calories | Protein | Sugar | Carbs

Dinner: _____
Calories | Protein | Sugar | Carbs

Thursday
Breakfast: _____
Calories | Protein | Sugar | Carbs

Lunch: _____
Calories | Protein | Sugar | Carbs

Dinner: _____
Calories | Protein | Sugar | Carbs

Friday
Breakfast: _____
Calories | Protein | Sugar | Carbs

Lunch: _____
Calories | Protein | Sugar | Carbs

Dinner: _____
Calories | Protein | Sugar | Carbs

Saturday
Breakfast: _____
Calories | Protein | Sugar | Carbs

Lunch: _____
Calories | Protein | Sugar | Carbs

Dinner: _____
Calories | Protein | Sugar | Carbs

Shopping List:
_____
_____
_____
_____
_____
_____
_____
_____

Noted:

WEEKLY MEAL PLANNING

Month: _____
Week: ① ② ③ ④

Sunday
Breakfast: _____
Calories | Protein | Sugar | Carbs

Lunch: _____
Calories | Protein | Sugar | Carbs

Dinner: _____
Calories | Protein | Sugar | Carbs

Monday
Breakfast: _____
Calories | Protein | Sugar | Carbs

Lunch: _____
Calories | Protein | Sugar | Carbs

Dinner: _____
Calories | Protein | Sugar | Carbs

Tuesday
Breakfast: _____
Calories | Protein | Sugar | Carbs

Lunch: _____
Calories | Protein | Sugar | Carbs

Dinner: _____
Calories | Protein | Sugar | Carbs

Wednesday
Breakfast: _____
Calories | Protein | Sugar | Carbs

Lunch: _____
Calories | Protein | Sugar | Carbs

Dinner: _____
Calories | Protein | Sugar | Carbs

Thursday
Breakfast: _____
Calories | Protein | Sugar | Carbs

Lunch: _____
Calories | Protein | Sugar | Carbs

Dinner: _____
Calories | Protein | Sugar | Carbs

Friday
Breakfast: _____
Calories | Protein | Sugar | Carbs

Lunch: _____
Calories | Protein | Sugar | Carbs

Dinner: _____
Calories | Protein | Sugar | Carbs

Saturday
Breakfast: _____
Calories | Protein | Sugar | Carbs

Lunch: _____
Calories | Protein | Sugar | Carbs

Dinner: _____
Calories | Protein | Sugar | Carbs

Shopping List:

Noted:

WEEKLY MEAL PLANNING

Month:
Week: (1) (2) (3) (4)

Sunday
Breakfast:
Calories Protein Sugar Carbs

Lunch:
Calories Protein Sugar Carbs

Dinner:
Calories Protein Sugar Carbs

Monday
Breakfast:
Calories Protein Sugar Carbs

Lunch:
Calories Protein Sugar Carbs

Dinner:
Calories Protein Sugar Carbs

Tuesday
Breakfast:
Calories Protein Sugar Carbs

Lunch:
Calories Protein Sugar Carbs

Dinner:
Calories Protein Sugar Carbs

Wednesday
Breakfast:
Calories Protein Sugar Carbs

Lunch:
Calories Protein Sugar Carbs

Dinner:
Calories Protein Sugar Carbs

Thursday
Breakfast:
Calories Protein Sugar Carbs

Lunch:
Calories Protein Sugar Carbs

Dinner:
Calories Protein Sugar Carbs

Friday
Breakfast:
Calories Protein Sugar Carbs

Lunch:
Calories Protein Sugar Carbs

Dinner:
Calories Protein Sugar Carbs

Saturday
Breakfast:
Calories Protein Sugar Carbs

Lunch:
Calories Protein Sugar Carbs

Dinner:
Calories Protein Sugar Carbs

Shopping List:

Noted:

WEEKLY MEAL PLANNING

Month: _____
Week: _____
(1) (2) (3) (4)

Sunday
Breakfast: _____
Calories | Protein | Sugar | Carbs

Lunch: _____
Calories | Protein | Sugar | Carbs

Dinner: _____
Calories | Protein | Sugar | Carbs

Monday
Breakfast: _____
Calories | Protein | Sugar | Carbs

Lunch: _____
Calories | Protein | Sugar | Carbs

Dinner: _____
Calories | Protein | Sugar | Carbs

Tuesday
Breakfast: _____
Calories | Protein | Sugar | Carbs

Lunch: _____
Calories | Protein | Sugar | Carbs

Dinner: _____
Calories | Protein | Sugar | Carbs

Wednesday
Breakfast: _____
Calories | Protein | Sugar | Carbs

Lunch: _____
Calories | Protein | Sugar | Carbs

Dinner: _____
Calories | Protein | Sugar | Carbs

Thursday
Breakfast: _____
Calories | Protein | Sugar | Carbs

Lunch: _____
Calories | Protein | Sugar | Carbs

Dinner: _____
Calories | Protein | Sugar | Carbs

Friday
Breakfast: _____
Calories | Protein | Sugar | Carbs

Lunch: _____
Calories | Protein | Sugar | Carbs

Dinner: _____
Calories | Protein | Sugar | Carbs

Saturday
Breakfast: _____
Calories | Protein | Sugar | Carbs

Lunch: _____
Calories | Protein | Sugar | Carbs

Dinner: _____
Calories | Protein | Sugar | Carbs

Shopping List:

Noted:

WEEKLY MEAL PLANNING

Month: _____
Week: ① ② ③ ④

Sunday
Breakfast: _____
Calories Protein Sugar Carbs

Lunch: _____
Calories Protein Sugar Carbs

Dinner: _____
Calories Protein Sugar Carbs

Monday
Breakfast: _____
Calories Protein Sugar Carbs

Lunch: _____
Calories Protein Sugar Carbs

Dinner: _____
Calories Protein Sugar Carbs

Tuesday
Breakfast: _____
Calories Protein Sugar Carbs

Lunch: _____
Calories Protein Sugar Carbs

Dinner: _____
Calories Protein Sugar Carbs

Wednesday
Breakfast: _____
Calories Protein Sugar Carbs

Lunch: _____
Calories Protein Sugar Carbs

Dinner: _____
Calories Protein Sugar Carbs

Thursday
Breakfast: _____
Calories Protein Sugar Carbs

Lunch: _____
Calories Protein Sugar Carbs

Dinner: _____
Calories Protein Sugar Carbs

Friday
Breakfast: _____
Calories Protein Sugar Carbs

Lunch: _____
Calories Protein Sugar Carbs

Dinner: _____
Calories Protein Sugar Carbs

Saturday
Breakfast: _____
Calories Protein Sugar Carbs

Lunch: _____
Calories Protein Sugar Carbs

Dinner: _____
Calories Protein Sugar Carbs

Shopping List:

Noted:

WEEKLY MEAL PLANNING

Month: _____
Week: _____
(1)(2)(3)(4)

Sunday
Breakfast: _____
Calories | Protein | Sugar | Carbs
[ ] [ ] [ ] [ ]

Lunch: _____
Calories | Protein | Sugar | Carbs
[ ] [ ] [ ] [ ]

Dinner: _____
Calories | Protein | Sugar | Carbs
[ ] [ ] [ ] [ ]

Monday
Breakfast: _____
Calories | Protein | Sugar | Carbs
[ ] [ ] [ ] [ ]

Lunch: _____
Calories | Protein | Sugar | Carbs
[ ] [ ] [ ] [ ]

Dinner: _____
Calories | Protein | Sugar | Carbs
[ ] [ ] [ ] [ ]

Tuesday
Breakfast: _____
Calories | Protein | Sugar | Carbs
[ ] [ ] [ ] [ ]

Lunch: _____
Calories | Protein | Sugar | Carbs
[ ] [ ] [ ] [ ]

Dinner: _____
Calories | Protein | Sugar | Carbs
[ ] [ ] [ ] [ ]

Wednesday
Breakfast: _____
Calories | Protein | Sugar | Carbs
[ ] [ ] [ ] [ ]

Lunch: _____
Calories | Protein | Sugar | Carbs
[ ] [ ] [ ] [ ]

Dinner: _____
Calories | Protein | Sugar | Carbs
[ ] [ ] [ ] [ ]

Thursday
Breakfast: _____
Calories | Protein | Sugar | Carbs
[ ] [ ] [ ] [ ]

Lunch: _____
Calories | Protein | Sugar | Carbs
[ ] [ ] [ ] [ ]

Dinner: _____
Calories | Protein | Sugar | Carbs
[ ] [ ] [ ] [ ]

Friday
Breakfast: _____
Calories | Protein | Sugar | Carbs
[ ] [ ] [ ] [ ]

Lunch: _____
Calories | Protein | Sugar | Carbs
[ ] [ ] [ ] [ ]

Dinner: _____
Calories | Protein | Sugar | Carbs
[ ] [ ] [ ] [ ]

Saturday
Breakfast: _____
Calories | Protein | Sugar | Carbs
[ ] [ ] [ ] [ ]

Lunch: _____
Calories | Protein | Sugar | Carbs
[ ] [ ] [ ] [ ]

Dinner: _____
Calories | Protein | Sugar | Carbs
[ ] [ ] [ ] [ ]

Shopping List:
_____
_____
_____
_____
_____
_____
_____
_____
_____
_____

Noted:

WEEKLY MEAL PLANNING

Month: _____
Week: _____
(1)(2)(3)(4)

Sunday
Breakfast: _____
Calories | Protein | Sugar | Carbs

Lunch: _____
Calories | Protein | Sugar | Carbs

Dinner: _____
Calories | Protein | Sugar | Carbs

Monday
Breakfast: _____
Calories | Protein | Sugar | Carbs

Lunch: _____
Calories | Protein | Sugar | Carbs

Dinner: _____
Calories | Protein | Sugar | Carbs

Tuesday
Breakfast: _____
Calories | Protein | Sugar | Carbs

Lunch: _____
Calories | Protein | Sugar | Carbs

Dinner: _____
Calories | Protein | Sugar | Carbs

Wednesday
Breakfast: _____
Calories | Protein | Sugar | Carbs

Lunch: _____
Calories | Protein | Sugar | Carbs

Dinner: _____
Calories | Protein | Sugar | Carbs

Thursday
Breakfast: _____
Calories | Protein | Sugar | Carbs

Lunch: _____
Calories | Protein | Sugar | Carbs

Dinner: _____
Calories | Protein | Sugar | Carbs

Friday
Breakfast: _____
Calories | Protein | Sugar | Carbs

Lunch: _____
Calories | Protein | Sugar | Carbs

Dinner: _____
Calories | Protein | Sugar | Carbs

Saturday
Breakfast: _____
Calories | Protein | Sugar | Carbs

Lunch: _____
Calories | Protein | Sugar | Carbs

Dinner: _____
Calories | Protein | Sugar | Carbs

Shopping List:

Noted:

Printed in Dunstable, United Kingdom